Sky Quake

by Thorvald Berthelsen

زلزال سماوي

توفارلد بيرتلسن

Sky Quake

Translated to English by Thorvald Berthelsen and Helge Krarup

Translated to Arabic by Alan Pary

First published in 2020 by CYBERWIT.NET® in India—HIG 45 KAUSHAMBI KUNJ, KALINDIPURAM, ALLAHABAD - 211011 (U.P.) India.

ISBN: 978-93-90202-48-5

Printed at Thomson Press India Limited.

In poetry you only occupy places you
leave, creating only works that you
release, you only achieve lasting time
by destroying time

René Char

في الشعر يبقى البقاء فقط في اماكن تغادرها، ولا
تخلق سوى أعمال تطلقها، يتحقق هذا فقط في وقت
طويل و عن طريق تدمير الوقت.

ـ رينيه شار

Katharsis

I often dream I
wake up with full clarity
and wake up in chaos

نقاء

غالباً احلم
استيقظ بوضوح كامل
و استفيق مع الكارثة

Daily moment

Trembling presence
at an expected passing
Everyday eternity

الآن و كل يوم

حضور متجانس
بخصوص موت منتظر
أبدية يومية

Not personal

The death of a loved one
The features blurred in
obstinate breath

غير شخصي

موت الحبيب
يتم محي تحركاته
بتنفس عنيد

Death's Head

Yawning bones
Weathered by birds kisses
Moth´s longing

الجمجمة

عظام تحدق
تتشرد قبلات الطيور
حنين فراشة الليل

Discouraged

Without touch, locked
in fantasy loops,
bloodied against open door

استسلام

بدون تلامس
محصور في الخيال
أنقل الدم الى باب مفتوح

Zero

At never o'clock
drops of chances
erode the white sun

الصفر

الساعة تدل الى اللاشيء
تتآكل خيارات التقطر
في شموس بيضاء

Behind the Looking Glass

In a place where nobody
wants to be grass is meeting
butterfly scales

خلف المرآة

في مكان ما
لا أحد يريد لقاء العشب
غبار الفراشات

Time is tight

The fish takes the clock
in the breast pocket of the clouds.
Only rain on the pane

ضيق الوقت

السمكة تأخذ على مدار الساعة
من الجيب الأمامي للغيوم
فقط المطر على النافذة

Lunacy

The coots restlessness
as if tomorrow will come.
Ripples in a pond

جنون

اضطرابات الغرّة
كما لو كان الغد موجودا
تموجات في البركة

Wishfull dreaming

Goutweed wildly grows
We hang it – in bloom – amongst
shooting stars on the wall

أمنية حلم

عشبة مظرة تنمو بسرعة
نجعلها تتشابك بين الزهرة
جدار من الشهاب

The gravity of Dreams

The dream fails in
taking off so it's pulling
the earth to heaven

أحلام الجاذبية

الحلم لديه صعوبة
بالتحليق
لذا يشّد الأرض الى السماء

Harbour Café

The fjord cuts into
sausages with evening sun
at odds with darkness

مقهى المرفأ

نهاية المضيق تؤدي
الى النقانق مع غروب الشمس
على حافة الظلام

The Riddle of Life Solved

We are material thrown
by the universe without
waste separation

حل لغز الحياة

نحن مادة رمينا
من قبل الكون
بدون تصفية النفايات

Sight/Insight

Glowing in the dark
the future of the past glistens
in a stranger's eye

البصر / البصيرة

يتوهج في الظلام
ماضي المستقبل
يرنو في عين الغريب

Everyday Failure:

Shipwrecked kisses
cannot sink for wayward
and errant wings

فشل يومي

قبلة المحطمين
لا يمكن أن تغرق
لأجنحة المخطئين

Fossil of Memory

Really to share
the moment before language
instantly becomes something else

تذكار احفوري

أجزاء حقيقية
لحظات قبل اللغة
يحدث على الفور شيء آخر

Shadow Play

The blue Moonshade
colors your dark skin red
in the prism of time

حركة الظل

ظل القمر الأزرق
يطلي سواد جلدك بالأحمر
في وحدة الوقت

News from Oz
Monkeys now fly by
not very perfect
as absence

No see, no hear
no nothing no tale

القردة الثلاث

القِردة تطير الآن
لا مزيد من الكمال
يمرون كالغائب

عميٌّ، صمُّ
لاشئ، لا حكاية

Reverse
King Midas' craving
for the dust of butterflies
turns the world around

العكس

رغبات الملک ميداس
لغبار الفراشات
تجول العالم

Misspelling
Selected loneliness
is regularly texted along with
wiper whisper

خطأ املائي

عزلة اختيارية
يتم ارسال رسائل قصيرة باتظام
الى همس النافذة

Dawn

The city bears fruit
in baskets of empty hands
that opens the dark

الفجر

المدينة تحمل الفواكه
في سلة من أيدى فارغة
سوف يحل الظلام

My Window
The colors are toned down
to almost black and white prints
by snow and hard frost

نافذتي

تخفت الألون
على طبعة شبه أبيض و أسود
الى الثلج و قساوة الصقيع

Breathe
The Moon hesitates
in expiration of the summer
between two stools

نفس

القمر يتردد
من زفير الصيف
بين كرسيين

Angel´s Pollen
Everyday angels -
like bumblebees – don't know
they can't fly

غبار الملائكة

ملائكة الأيام
لا تعرف مثل النحل
بأنها لا تستطيع الطيران

Our Time

In dreams before
they are dreamt we move
into each other

Clocks melt down
through ordinary life
in today's promise

وقتنا

في الأحلام
قبل حدوث الحلم
نتحرك مع بعضنا البعض

الساعة تذوب
مع مرورو الأيام
الى يوم الميعاد

Time of the Stone
No more time
The rain crackling on stone
Clouds being hollowed

العصر الحجري

لا مزيد من الوقت
المطر يطحن الحجر
الغيوم تتآكل

Night Vision
I hear clouds and
see the thin screams of mice
Night everywhere

رؤية ليلية

أسمع الغيوم
و أرى صراخ الفأر
الرطوبة في كل مكان

Glade

Moss embrace stones
the shadow feeds the roots
dazzled by the moon

جفاء

الطحلب يعانق الحجر
الظل يغذي الجذور
انبهار من القمر

Utopia backwards
Autumn dreams
Water's biological clock
Digital plankton

اليوتوبيا من الخلف

أحلام الخريف
الساعة البيولوجية للمياه
العوالق الرقمية

Insight
The room expands
infinitely curling
up in itself

The puddle reflects
selfdevouring the heaven
without windows

المعرفة

الغرفة تتوسع
انحناء بلا حدود
مع ذواتها

انعكاسات الماء
سماء تلتهم نفسها
بدون نوافذ

Purposeless
Slow rockslide
Thaw the rest of life
without a new direction

بلا هدف

انهيار صخري بطئ
يصطدم لبقية الحياة
بدون مأوى جديد

Dam Collapse
Dripping water damage
burdening the ceiling in the dream
which is a tidal wave

حطام السد

قطرات اضرار المياه
يضغط على السقوف في الحلم
مثل موجة عارمة

Thaw
Dripping moonbuds
streaks of rain in the vision
growth as abscesses

تغير مفاجيء

القمر تتقطر منه البراعم
بقايا المطر الغير مرئي
طبقات تنمو بتلعثم

Clarification

Fog on the fjord inlet
The water mirror clearing up
ready for the sky

تغير مناخي

ضباب عبر النهر
مرآة المياه الصافية
على استعداد للسماء

Biology?

Horny without
awareness of the goal
Buds under snow

علم الأحياء؟

القيادة في
اللاوعي نحو الهدف
برعم تحت الثلج

Rainbow Bridge
On the rainbow bridge
between dream and reality
unrest crosses

جسر من قوز قزح

على جسر من قوز قزح
بين الحلم و الواقع
يزول الأضطراب

Widened
Circling gulls
open up the horizon
through screams of time

التمدد

النوارس تطوف
يفتح الأفق
من خلال صرخة الوقت

Flight of Thoughts
The shuttling of trains
through dead zones of text-messages
aphorisms of fields

افكار شاردة

مسيرة مكوكية
عبر رسائل القصيرة لمنطقة الموت
لتعبير متمركز

Hocus Crocus
The cemetery snow
melts into crocus puddles
someone can walk on

معجزة

ثلوج المقبرة
تذوب في ندى الزعفران
شخص ما يسير عليه

On Poles
In the labia
of oyster stone the tongue
falls out of the words

على الأقطاب

في بنكرياس المحار
يسقط اللسان
من الكلمات

The Fragrance of Silence

The sharpness of lilacs
in the echoes of hospital corridors
losses muted by felt

Again I fall asleep
over the pain solitaires
that never comes out

We are burning inside
with the spark which anyway does not
go out on its own

رائحة الصمت

الحدة من الأحماض
في أصداء ممرات المستشفى
خسارة أوتار خافتة

النعاس من جديد
على الألم المنفرد
الذي لا يمحي

نحن نحترق في الداخل
على أية حال بكل تألق
لا تخرج لوحدك

Lacking Perspective in the Loss

The quiet change
of need to self-reflecting
failure of conscience

مسار مفقود

هدوء متناوب
بحاجة للضمير
انعكاس فشل ذاتي

Everyday loss
Losing the face
in a shiny worn out kimono´s
mirroring of the day

خسارات يومية

وصمة عار
على قميص شبه لامع
مرآة على مر اليوم

Call

My new cell phone,
cut out from The Dreaming –
Bzzz, from when, where

مكالمة

هاتفي المحمول الجديد
قد انفصل بمرور وقت الحلم
بييززززز، منذ متى، أين؟

Glowing Fire
Glows in the dark
future of the past flicker for
the wind of uncertainty

توهج النار

لهيب في العتمة
ماضي المستقبل يضرب
برياح الشك

Love Focus
The cunt's wave suction
around the dick flanks – focus
outgrows us, now

تركيز الحب

حتكاك سائل المهبل
يلتفت حول مسار القضيب ـ التركيز
ينمو منا الآن

Love Mirror
Love finds bones
and genomes
in its dreams

مرآة الحب

الحب يجد
العظام و كتل وراثية
في حلمه

Poem about nourishment
The poem does not
understand humans.
Does the umbilical cord?

شعر حول التغذية

الشعر لا يقتنع
بالناس
هل يشعر به الحبل السري؟

Still Life
Hang silence up -
with the head on one side
I see my heartbeat

على قدم وساق

الصمت معلق
مائلاً من رأسه
أرى نبضات القلب

Kite on a leash*
Rolling up darkness
around the loose grip of longings
in the kite´s tail
* A kite means Flying Dragon in Denmark.

حبل طائرة الورقية*

الضلام يدامس
على اشتياق مسكة غير موفقة
لذيل التنين

*طائرة ورقيه تعنى التنين الطائر بالدنماركييه.

Evening sun
Presence of time
in moss on rocks and violet
knowledge of lakes

شمس المساء

حضور مع الوقت
منخفض على الصخور و البحيرات
معرفة بنفسجية

Present
Are souls unthinkable
without people
that goes up and down each other
longing for presence
                    Marianne Larsen

Lovingly longing for
each other, best at the same time
without it being felt

الحاضر

الروح لا تفكر
بدون اناس تتفارق بعضهم البعض
اشتياق للحضور
ـ ماريانا لارسن

اشتياق عزيز
للبعض
يفضل ان يكون بنفس الوقت لا شعورياً

Certain Knowledge

65% of Danes think that everything is
the fault of imams. An even greater
number believe that socialism of any
kind has proven its uselessness. I got a
used welded red bike for my 5th
birthday, but it could not bear to run
against a wall

My first bike
collapsed, run against a wall
Red's no good at all

يالها من معلومة

٦٥% من الدنماركيين يحملون العبأ للمسلمين.
أغلبهم يرون أن الأجتماعيين كان لديهم علم بهذا
الدمار. لقد استلمت دراجة حمراء في يوم عيد
ميلادي، التي لم تتحمل اندحارها نحو الجدار.

دراجتي الأولى انكسرت
تدحرجت صوب الجدار
الاحمر ليس جيدا على الاطلاق

Rebirth
Sorrow's crazy egg
have the umbilical cord
cut and flows out, tough

ولادة جديدة

حزن بيضة مجنونة
يقطع حبلها السري
و تتدفق، ياالروعة

Night Vision
No wing strokes
on the back of the moon the
sand painting of light

رؤية ليلية

لا هبة في الريح
من خلف القمر
النور لوحة رملية

Underground
Mushrooms late summer
The rain cleans the sky
mycelia grow

تحت الأرض

حواس الفطر
المطر ينظف السماء
غزلها ينمو

Realtime
To drown and burn
in the holeow world's dream
about an eternal now

الوقت الحقيقي

الأختناق و الحريق
في العالم الأبيض للحلم
حول خلود آني

Castles in the Sky?
The spiral calm of clouds
we build from the bottom of
air volcanoes

قلاع الهواء؟

هدوء لولب السماء
نبني من القاع
لبراكين الهواء

Insanely limpid
Behind the wall of glass the
spin doctor of the moon is
finding his proper shadow

نقاء زجاج جنوني

وراء جدار من الزجاج
مستشار القمر
يجد ظله الحقيقي

Stumbling near
The shadow differs
from darkness and settles
at my feet

قرابة متعثرة

الظل ينفصل
عن الظلمة
و يتواجد بين اقدامي

Slippery Slope
The narrow view of the inclined window
through sky and roofs
keeps the balance

مخطوطة مائلة

جزء من النافذة المائلة
بين السماء و السقف
يركن التوازن

Cord Linkage

Between dust and kisses
red ribbons are bound damn´d
unbearably loose

الآلية

بين القبلة و الغبار
تربط الأشرطة الحمراء بأحكام
حيث فكها يكون صعبا

Network
The blind trust of
the mayfly in the flame mains
The one click eternity

الشبكة

عمي فراشات يومية
تثق بنور الحريق
نقرة للخلود

Finally
Silent language
of clouds in blueing punctuation
of infinity

و أخيراً

لغة صمت الغيوم
في تنقيط ازرق
ما لانهاية

Weave

Lies and betrayal
of Silk is holding on to death
in this poem cocoon

نسيج

كذب الحرير و انخذل
تمسك وجاهة بالموت
في شرنقة القصيدة

Expiration
The homeless poem
in furious distance from
itself and the present

انتهاء

الشعر بلا مأوى
في مسافة غاضبة
من نفسه و من اللحظة

Caligraphy
Bird signs in the wind
Almost understandable
just before – well now

جمالية الكتابة

طيور في الريح
بفهم تقريبي
قبل الآن ـ حسناآ الآن

The light
Life's calm flame
unreasonable safety to the
sound of assassination

الضوء

شعلة الحياة الهادئة
آمنة بشكل غير معقول
لصوت الأغتيال

Nirvana
In the forgetting night
my fatigue is transported
easier than hope

السكينة

في ليلة منسية
ينقل تعبي
اسهل من الأمل

Glass Moon

Glass moon on snow
Raw sake lobotomy
brutalizes the day

زجاج القمر

زجاج القمر على الثلج
بقايا خدش البياض
يوم خالي من الوجدان

Absent Caresses
From fainted
mobile phones sighing
grows your presence

المداعبات المطلقة

من اغماء
تتنهد المحمول
ينمو وجودك

Time
Sparklers
spread atomized darkness
The lobotomy of Light years

الوقت

نجوم متلألئة
تنتشر في غبار الظلمة
سنوات ضوئية لخدش البياض

Everyday of the Dream
The breath of sleep
awakes childhood´s eyes
on the everyday of dreams

أيام الحلم

يتنفس النوم
تستيقظ عيون الطفولة
في أيام الحلم

Amalfi
The pride of lemons
on bent fresh shots
out in the blue mist

أمالفي*

ثقة الليمون
فوق انحناءات معصورة
في نقطة زرقاء

*أمالفي: بلدية في مقاطعة ساليرنو في أيطاليا

Oleanders over
photos of Mussolini
a child on the boot

زهرة الدفلي
تتكاثر أمام صورة موسوليني
مع اطفال في الأحذية

"We are making
paper nothing but paper
of old rags"

" نحن نصنع الورق
ولا شيء غير ثياب قديمة
نصنع"

Police ensures
that all unbuttoned shirts
are buttoned up

الشرطة تضمن
جميع القمصان المفتوحة
تتم بغلقها

Navigation Rules
in the evening rush hour
set new tracks

قوانين الملاحة
في المساء
يحدد مسارات جديدة

A smart chick cuts
her nails on the sneakers
in the Knight's slipstream**

**The Italian ex government chief, mass media
owner and billionaire Berlusconi's nickname is the
Knight

ذكاء منحدرات الرنجة
أظافر تخرج من الأحذية الرياضية
في سرعة الفارس**

** الرئيس السابق الأيطالي و مالك الأعلام الجماهيري و
المليار دير الأول برلسكوني هو الفارس.

The man who does not
lie on the corner, folds
a cardboard bed for the night

الرجل الذي
لا يستلقي في الزاوية
يسحب الكارتونة من الليل

The red moon
is in a rush against time
clearly in outbreak

القمر الأحمر
مندفعآ أمام الزمن
واضحآ تماما في الكارثة

The dream wakes up
Absence of clouds in
the bankers smoky gray hesitation
never fill up

يستيقظ الحلم

الغيوم تهرب من

شدة دخان رمادي لرجل المصرف

لا يمتلأ التردد أبدآ

Commemorative Shift
The flash of memory
bursts the pearlescent of clams
in slippery on water

The Chinese Box
reversed - opens in a flash

ذاكرة الجهتين

ذاكرة الزمن
تهب على أم اللؤلؤ
في تراب على الماء

الصندوق الصيني
يعكس ـ يفتح من الآن

I am the poet who carries along the dried-up wells, that you fill from afar, my love.

René Char

أنا الشاعر الذي اجلب آبار المجففة، انت يا حبي
بمسافة تملئيها.

ــ رينه شار

Game of Hearts
As adult children on
four lids we slide naked
in a game of tag

through abandoned homes where we
thought no one was caught

حرية قلب

كالأطفال البالغين
مع اربعة قفازات
ننزلق عراة على السقوف

بين المنازل المهجورة
التى كنا نضن أن لا احد يسكنها

Tread air
Here we can't touch
bottom, just excite the blood
to gasp after gasp

دخول الهواء

هنا لا نسطتيع نبقى بالأسفل
فقط آثار الدم
للحظات تلوة لحظات

The bottom line
We hang in kisses
That are life-distance close
encounters to such an extent

بالمختصر المفيد

نشتبك بالقبلة
قريبين من مسافة الحياة
متصلين لهذا الحد

Breaking up
We are walking through moorland
between quivering heights
of the smoldering mist

أنفكاك

نحن ذاهبون الى الحاضر
بين اشتعال الضباب
ارتفاعات عالية

Collapse
Glossed off future
Tectonic plates of skin
tear the world open

انكسار

مجد المستقبل
صفائح الجلد التكتونية
يتمزق العالم المباح

Fleeing Flight
Fear falls in my back
The future flees forward
without footprints

هروب الهارب

الخوف من الخيانه
يهرب المستقبل الى الأمام
بدون أثر

Melt Down
Nature melts
us over the head – even
the grave disappears

انصهار من جديد

الطبيعة تنصهر
نحن على الرأس ــ حتى
القبر يختفي

Insulation

We are so close
that the air membrane quiver
in the wave ridge of our bones

انعزال

نحن مقتربون جدا
ان غشاء الهواء يهتز
في احتراق العظام

Disappearances and reappearances
My nostrils just now
are dilated in the world's fragrance
You have passed by

الأختفاء و المجيء ثانية

شقوق الأنف
تنتفخ في عطر العالم
أنت مررت من هنا

Round-shouldered Powerlessness
With the back against
headwinds, we turn the world to
get used to tailwind

الأنحناء بقوة

نعطي ظهرنا
لرياح قاسية
نقلب العالم الى رياح عاتية

Drive

Between the words
the undercurrents are
recharging hunger

أشتغال

بين الأحرف
هناك اتجاهات خفية
تشحن الجوع من جديد

Aqua vitae
The eye of the well
gives the night the light that spreads
out the universe

In everything
cracks let life in and out
pure chemistry of water

سيرة الذاتية للماء

عين البئر تعطي
ضوء الليل
على نطاق واسع في الكون

ينشق في كل شيء
حياة تدخل و تنطلق
الماء كيمياء صافي

Evening Outbreak
Twilight's echo
Swing of swallows and bats
Black lightning strikes up

تفشي المساء

صدى الشفق
انحنائات الطائر و الخفاش
برق أسود يحتضر

The Offspring
Winter does not know
what it jumps into
flowers are flowering

المصدر

الشتاء لا يعرف
ما هو مصدر
انفتاح الورود

Sky Quake

A tone, yellow
and warm, shakes all horizons
in my foundations

زلزال سماوي

ومضة صفراء دافئة
تهتز الآفاق كلها
تحت أعماقي

www.ingramcontent.com/pod-product-compliance
Lightning Source LLC
Chambersburg PA
CBHW031343160726
47993CB00002B/817